ULTIMATE STICKER BOOK

STAR WARS
REBELS™

REBEL ADVENTURES

How to use this book

Read the captions, then find the sticker that best fits the space.
(hint: check the sticker labels for clues!)

•

Don't forget that your stickers
can be stuck down and peeled off again.

•

There are lots of fantastic extra stickers too!

DK

LONDON, NEW YORK,
MELBOURNE, MUNICH AND DELHI

Written and edited by David Fentiman and Sadie Smith
Designed by Anna Formanek
Additional design by Elena Jarmoskaite

With special thanks to Jonathan W. Rinzler, Troy Alders,
Leland Chee and Carol Roeder at Lucasfilm.

Published in Great Britain by
Dorling Kindersley Ltd,
80 Strand, London, WC2R 0RL

10 9 8 7 6 5 4
001—268745—Aug/14

A CIP catalogue record for this book is available from the British Library.

ISBN: 978-1-40935-651-6

Colour reproduction by Alta Image, UK
Printed and bound by L. Rex Printing Co. Ltd, China

Discover more at
www.dk.com
www.starwars.com

THE PLANET LOTHAL

The peaceful world of Lothal was conquered by the Empire many years ago. The planet's mineral resources were mined, the land was polluted and huge factories were built to make weapons for the Imperial Army. The people of Lothal now suffer under the Empire's brutal rule.

A valuable world

The Empire was attracted to Lothal by its rich mineral resources and its location on an important route through hyperspace.

Imperial rule

The Empire stamps down hard on any signs of rebellion. Cruel Imperial agents arrest anyone who complains about Imperial laws.

Stormtroopers

Stormtroopers are soldiers of the Empire. They have been sent to Lothal to keep the people of the planet under control.

The resistance

Not everyone on Lothal is willing to let the Empire rule their planet. One small band of rebels is determined to free their world!

Sinister skies
In addition to stormtroopers, TIE fighters of the Imperial Navy are based on Lothal. They hunt down smugglers and troublemakers.

Paradise lost
The beautiful plains of Lothal are being ruined forever by the Empire. Its mines and factories are turning the land into a poisoned wilderness.

The underworld
The Empire's harsh rule has created a thriving black market on Lothal. Shady gangsters like Cikatro Vizago sell people what they need... for a heavy price.

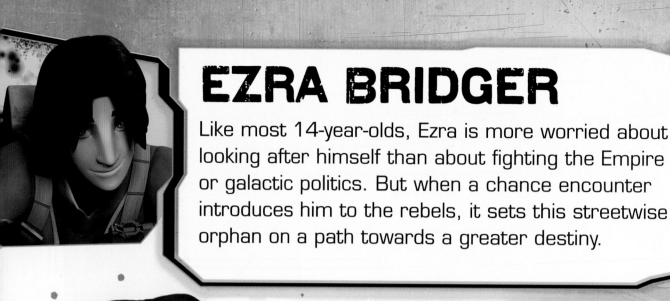

EZRA BRIDGER

Like most 14-year-olds, Ezra is more worried about looking after himself than about fighting the Empire or galactic politics. But when a chance encounter introduces him to the rebels, it sets this streetwise orphan on a path towards a greater destiny.

Ezra's tower
Ezra lives alone inside an old abandoned communications tower. It stands in the countryside outside Lothal's Capital City.

Feeling the Force
Ezra has amazing reflexes, but he never realised that he could sense the Force. This is the mysterious energy field that gives Jedi their powers.

Ezra and Chopper

Ezra's relationship with Chopper is rough. They constantly play pranks on each other, but Chopper enjoys the attention Ezra gives him.

Rookie rebel

When Ezra first joins the rebels, he is used to looking only after himself. To begin with, he finds it hard to work as part of a team.

Tech collector

Living as an orphan, Ezra has to find a way to feed himself. He uses his street skills to steal technology, which he then sells on the black market.

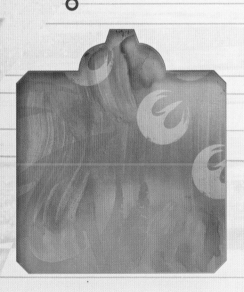

Jedi apprentice

Kanan agrees to take Ezra on as his Jedi apprentice. He is Kanan's first pupil.

Ezra's lightsaber

When Kanan thinks that Ezra is ready, they travel on a dangerous quest together. They must find a vital part Ezra needs to build his own lightsaber.

HERA SYNDULLA

Hera is an ace pilot and a crucial member of the rebel team. She flies them on their missions and gets everyone home safely afterwards. She cares deeply about her crewmates, and believes passionately in the rebel cause, but she also has a hidden, mysterious side.

Rebel Twi'lek

Hera is a Twi'lek from the planet Ryloth. Her homeworld has also been occupied by the Empire, and her people suffer terribly under the Empire's control.

Friendly advice

Kanan leads the rebels when they go into battle, but Hera is always there to give him guidance on important decisions.

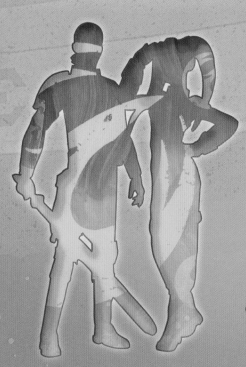

Crack shot

Hera keeps a secret blaster in her boot. If a situation becomes dangerous, she is a crack shot with it.

Kanan and Hera

Kanan and Hera are very close. It was Hera who convinced Kanan to become a rebel. Together they act as mentors to the younger members of the group.

Flying ace

Hera's piloting skills are top-notch, and she often manages to outfly and shoot down Imperial TIE fighters.

The *Ghost*

Hera's ship is called the *Ghost*. The *Ghost* looks like a normal freighter, but it has special weapons and hidden defences.

KANAN JARRUS

Kanan leads the rebels as their general, commanding their missions against the Empire. He was a young Jedi apprentice at the end of the Clone Wars, when most of the Jedi were wiped out by the Empire. He escaped, and alongside Hera he created the rebel group on Lothal.

Hidden Jedi
Kanan tries not to show his Jedi abilities in public. He knows that the Empire is always on the look-out for those with Force powers.

Rebel recruiter
Kanan sees that Ezra has a lot of potential, and that the Force is strong with him. He persuades Ezra to join the rebels in their struggle.

Jedi mentor
Kanan doesn't like to talk about his past life as a Jedi, but after realising Ezra can feel the Force, Kanan must remember his own Jedi training if he is to teach the boy.

Kanan's lightsaber
Kanan must be careful about using his lightsaber. He usually keeps it on board the *Ghost*, and uses it only when he has to.

Kanan's blaster
In most situations, a blaster is Kanan's weapon of choice. It may not be as graceful as a lightsaber, but it attracts much less attention.

ZEB

Garazeb "Zeb" Orrelios is a strong fighter with a very personal hatred of the Empire. His massive body makes him a powerful brawler, and he's usually happiest when he's punching stormtroopers. When the rebels are outnumbered, they can count on Zeb to even the score.

Lonely Lasat

Zeb is a Lasat. His race was nearly wiped out by the Empire when they invaded his homeworld of Lasan. There are few Lasat left in the galaxy.

Alien with attitude

Zeb is brash and doesn't keep his opinions to himself. If he thinks a plan is stupid or pointless he will say so. Loudly.

Zeb's bo-rifle

Zeb's weapon is called a bo-rifle. It is both a fighting staff and a laser rifle. Bo-rifles are the traditional weapon of the Honor Guard of Lasan.

Zeb and Ezra

At first, Zeb doesn't think much of Ezra. Once Ezra proves himself though, Zeb becomes more like Ezra's older brother, and teases him constantly.

USE YOUR EXTRA
STICKERS TO CREATE
YOUR OWN SCENE.

SABINE WREN

Sabine is the group's explosives expert. She is also a skilled artist who loves decorating her crewmates' equipment. And her enemies' equipment. And their vehicles... She is a free spirit, who joined the rebels for excitement and adventure.

Mandalorian

Sabine's armour shows that she is a Mandalorian. On Mandalore, she learned the true nature of the Empire, and escaped to join the rebels.

Talented artist

Sabine will paint anything she can get her hands on. Her clothes are always covered in paint from her latest creations.

Explosives expert

Sabine makes all of her explosives by hand. When they explode they usually cover anything nearby with paint!

Sabine's blasters

Sabine is a great shot with her twin blasters. Just like everything else, she has decorated them with her own unique style.

CHOPPER

C1-10P, a.k.a. "Chopper" is a cranky old astromech droid. Officially it's his job to help Hera pilot the *Ghost* and to repair the ship. In reality it's very hard to get Chopper to do anything, and he doesn't seem to like anyone – with the possible exception of Ezra.

Grumpy astromech

Chopper doesn't like taking orders. When the crew are in serious trouble he'll step in and save them, but certainly not because they ordered him to.

Patched together

No one is quite sure how old Chopper is, but he is *old*. He has been rebuilt so many times that he is now mostly spare parts.

Prank wars

Chopper's favourite game is playing pranks on Ezra. He will wait for the perfect moment to embarrass him, but Ezra always gets him back.

THE *GHOST*

The rebels' missions would be impossible without the *Ghost*. This old freighter is both their home, and their secret base. It carries them into battle and protects them when they are attacked by the Empire. The *Ghost* never lets the rebels down.

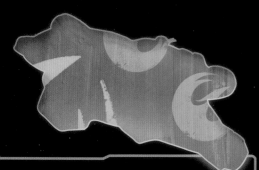

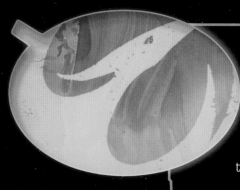

Laser cannons
The *Ghost* is heavily armed and can defend itself against most threats, but the rebels prefer to avoid space battles if they can.

Hidden base
The *Ghost* gets its name from its special systems that keep it hidden from Imperial sensors. These systems let the rebels move around undetected.

The *Phantom*
The *Ghost* is really two ships in one. The rear part disconnects as a separate shuttle, named the *Phantom*.

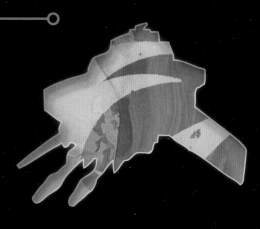

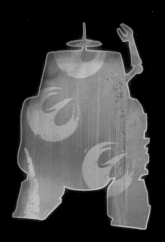

Fixing the ship
Chopper has been repairing the *Ghost* for a long time. He is now the only one who knows exactly how it is put together.

The cockpit
The *Ghost* has a roomy cockpit where the pilot and copilot sit side by side. The ship's forward laser cannons are fired from here.

USE YOUR EXTRA
STICKERS TO CREATE
YOUR OWN SCENE.

REBELS IN ACTION

The rebels may not have the mighty weapons or vast starships of the Empire, but they have a few tricks up their sleeves. Each of the rebels brings special skills to their missions, and the Empire has learned not to underestimate them!

The deadeye
When Ezra first joins the rebels, his main weapon is his energy slingshot. He uses it to shoot balls of energy accurately over long distances.

The brawler
Zeb likes to get up close in battle. He has powerful fists, and his bo-rifle transforms into a staff. This allows him to stun nearby stormtroopers.

The Jedi
When he needs to, Kanan uses his Jedi lightsaber. He can use it to deflect enemy laser blasts and cut through almost anything.

The pilot
Hera is most comfortable behind the controls of a spacecraft, but she isn't afraid of using her blaster when things get tough!

STICKERS

Stormtroopers

Rebel Twi'lek

Prank wars

Kanan and Hera

Feeling the Force

Laser cannons

The *Phantom*

Rebel recruiter

Tech collector

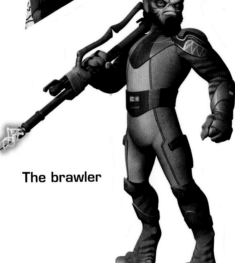

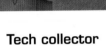

The brawler

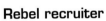

Alien with attitude

The pilot

STICKERS

Rookie rebel

The *Ghost*

Mandalorian

Zeb and Ezra

The resistance

Grumpy
astromech

Flying ace

The deadeye

Kanan's lightsaber

Hidden base

Ezra and Chopper

The underworld

STICKERS

Fixing the ship

The cockpit

Zeb's bo-rifle

A valuable world

Friendly advice

Kanan's blaster

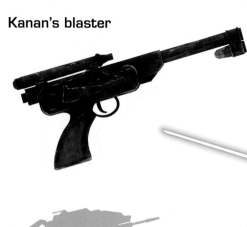

Jedi apprentice

Crack shot

STICKERS

Patched together

Paradise lost

Sabine's blasters

Ezra's lightsaber

Hidden Jedi

The Jedi

Explosives expert

Imperial rule

STICKERS

Jedi mentor

Sinister skies

Talented artist

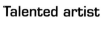

Ezra's tower

Lonely Lasat

EXTRA STICKERS